Unbelievable Pictures and Facts About Llamas

By: Olivia Greenwood

Introduction

Llamas look very similar to camels, although they do not have a hump. They are kind and gentle animals, that are loved by most people. Today we will be exploring the exciting world of llamas.

Exactly how are baby llamas born?

When a baby llama is born, all the females in the community surround the mother. This is for support and to ensure that no males or predators come near them.

On average how long is a female llama pregnant for?

The average amount of time that a female llama is pregnant for is around 11 months. This is actually longer than human beings are pregnant for.

What colors are llamas?

Llamas can be all sorts of colors, they generally are white to black with different shades and sports and they can even come in red, beige, brown or a combination of these colors.

What do llamas do to defend themselves?

Llamas have a fascinating way of spitting in order to defend themselves, they spit at each other when they are angry or upset, they may even spit at a human if you upset or provoke it.

Are llamas fast animals or not?

You won't believe this but llamas are extremely fast, when they want to they can move faster than humans can. You can't outrun a llama even if you tried very hard.

Are llamas a threat to humans?

Llamas are very gentle animals and they are not a threat to humans at all, unfortunately, humans can be a threat to them.

What does the llama generally symbolize?

The llama symbolizes a couple of things, but mainly it symbolizes independence, freedom, and strength.

Who are enemies of the llama?

Llamas have a couple of different enemies which include lions, cougars and unfortunately humans too.

Who is the domesticated cousin of the llama?

One of the most domesticated animals which are closely related to the llamas is an animal called the alpaca. They actually look very similar to llamas, so it is important to not confuse the two.

Is the wool of a llama used for anything specific?

Llamas have the most beautiful wool, which is used by people for many things, especially to make really warm and great luxurious clothing.

Are these animals easy to train or not?

It is very interesting to learn that llamas can get trained and they are easy to train mainly because they are calm and intelligent animals.

Are llamas smart animals?

Many people do not know this, but llamas are actually very smart animals and they are far from stupid.

On average how long do llamas generally live for?

Llamas are animals that can live a decent and long life, on average they can live for around 20 years.

What is the correct name for a baby llama?

The correct terminology which is used for a baby llama is a cria.

Are llamas social or solitary animals?

Llamas are wonderful animals who enjoy being together and socializing. They are far from solitary animals and they are certainly social animals.

On average how long have llamas been on earth for?

This may completely blow your mind, llamas have been on earth for over 40 million years, this is what the experts predict.

What types of food do llamas eat?

Firstly it may be important to know that llamas are considered to be herbivores. They eat a diet that is rich in leaves, plants, and grass.

What type of environments do llamas live in?

Llamas can be found in all different types of environments, which includes mountains, deserts, valleys, and grasslands.

How many different types of llamas are there in the world?

In general, there are actually two distinct types of llamas, one type is short-haired, while the other type is long-haired.

Which animal group do llamas belong to?

Llamas are very special animals and they belong to the animal class of mammals.

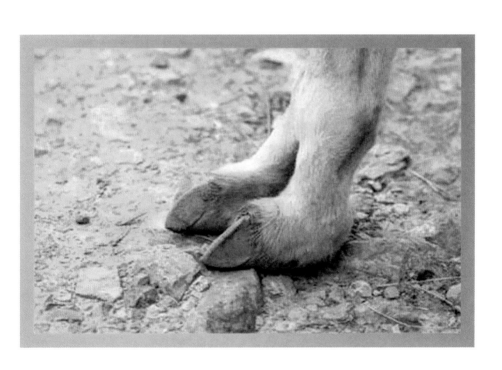

Made in the USA
San Bernardino, CA
11 December 2019